HANDLING STUDENT FRUSTRATIONS

How do I help students manage emotions in the classroom?

Renate **CAINE** | Carol **McCLINTIC**

ASCD Alexandria, VA USA

ASCD®
Website: www.ascd.org
E-mail: books@ascd.org

ASCD | arias™
www.ascdarias.org

Printed in the United States of America. Cover art © 2014 by ASCD. ASCD publications present a variety of viewpoints. The views expressed or implied in this book should not be interpreted as official positions of the Association.

ASCD LEARN TEACH LEAD® and ASCD ARIAS™ are trademarks owned by ASCD and may not be used without permission. All other referenced trademarks are the property of their respective owners.

PAPERBACK ISBN: 978-1-4166-1913-0   ASCD product #SF114068

Also available as an e-book (see Books in Print for the ISBNs).

Library of Congress Cataloging-in-Publication Data
Caine, Renate Nummela.
 Handling student frustrations : how do I help students manage emotions in the classroom? / Renate Caine and Carol McClintic.
    p. cm.
 Includes bibliographical references.
 ISBN 978-1-4166-1913-0 (pbk. : alk. paper) 1. Child psychology. 2. Educational psychology. 3. Emotions in children. 4. School environment—Psychological aspects. 5. Classroom management. I. Title.
 LB1117.C255 2014
 370.15—dc 3
                    2014006339

21 20 19 18 17 16 15 14   1 2 3 4 5 6 7 8 9 10

HANDLING STUDENT FRUSTRATIONS

How do I help students manage emotions in the classroom?

Want to earn a free ASCD Arias e-book?
Your opinion counts! Please take 2–3 minutes to give
us your feedback on this publication. All survey
respondents will be entered into a drawing to
win an ASCD Arias e-book.

Please visit
www.ascd.org/ariasfeedback

Thank you!

The APA Method

The elements of emotional intelligence—being aware of our feelings and handling disruptive emotions well, empathizing with how others feel, and being skillful in handling our relationships—are crucial abilities for effective living.

We should be teaching the basics of emotional intelligence in schools.

—Daniel Goleman

Parents, students, administrators, the public at large: most people don't understand the kind of pressure teachers are under on a daily basis. They face multiple demands, such as

- Meeting students' unique academic needs.
- Raising student test scores.
- Mastering the constant stream of new technology.
- Keeping up with continually shifting district and administrative requirements, including implementation of new standards.

In addition to these challenges, classrooms are filled with constant shifts and changes as students struggle to manage their day-to-day social and emotional needs. Family situations, peer relationships, and personal yearnings for acceptance and inclusion can, and often do, result in actions and reactions not easily dealt with or recognized. When students' frustrations erupt in the classroom, teachers need to be prepared to respond to them quickly and successfully. To that end, we have designed the Acknowledge/Process/Act (APA) method for helping you to create conditions that will result in better relationships with your students. Regardless of grade level, following the three steps of the method will result in higher student motivation and achievement:

- **Step 1: Acknowledge.** Help the student accept the situation, including his or her own reaction.
- **Step 2: Process.** As soon as time allows, help the student clarify what is actually taking place. Together with the student, come up with an action plan for moving forward.
- **Step 3: Act.** Help the student implement the action plan. This may sound simple, but it is possibly the most difficult and important step.

The APA process will help you to

- Handle everyday situations and emotional issues you encounter in your classroom.
- Implement strategies that can lead to a more peaceful, respectful, and productive learning environment.
- Understand how strongly negative emotions can override learning and sabotage academic goals.
- Identify triggers for emotional overload.

Our focus in these pages is on those students who function well most of the time, but who may temporarily be experiencing an emotional crisis—what we refer to as *hijacking*. When the brain is hijacked, students' emotional reactions can take over their thinking and make learning difficult if not impossible. They may also act out in ways that puzzle, frustrate, and, yes, infuriate both teachers and classmates.

All too often, teachers must deal with open defiance from students who willfully ignore established rules and agreements. As one young teacher recently told us, "90 percent of my time is spent dealing with emotional issues that have nothing to do with what I am supposed to be teaching." Most teachers still believe that they must manage and control how their students behave and learn. We believe strongly that educators should instead create positive and respectful relationships with students, but moving from control to collaboration is not easy.

The Science Behind the Hijacked Brain

The limbic system of the brain reacts to any real or imagined crisis by directly sending energy to the brain's survival system, which is in charge of securing the individual's immediate survival. This is known as the "fight or flight" response, during which cortisol, the stress hormone, is released into the bloodstream. As Daniel Goleman (2001), the author of *Emotional Intelligence*, says, "When cortisol levels are high, people make more errors, are more distracted, and can't remember as well. Irrelevant thoughts intrude, and processing information becomes more difficult" (p. 76). The brain is commonly hijacked in this way when we are faced with such scenarios as

- Having to constantly make decisions.
- Needing to deal with frequent changes.
- Continually rushing to meet constant deadlines and other time pressures.
- Being unprepared to deal with personal conflicts and challenges.

The Continuum of Emotional States

An emotional state is defined by the level of real or imagined threat that an individual senses. Bruce Perry (2003), a neuroscientist at the Trauma Center at Baylor University in Austin, Texas, has devised a continuum showing how emotions are tied to physiological states. Because emotions affect our physiologies, they help determine what parts of the brain are most active and accessible at a given moment. In rising order of intensity, Perry's continuum of emotional states is as follows: *calm, arousal, alarm,* and *fear.* Each of these states determines what areas of an individual's brain are predominantly active, how well or what kind of thinking an individual is capable of, and what kind of behavior can be expected:

- **Calm.** When we are calm, we can be engaged—we can plan, find solutions, and think creatively and abstractly. Creative and abstract thinking are essential for mastering strong emotions.
- **Arousal.** In this state of heightened vigilance, we tend to focus on such concrete aspects of learning as how much time is needed, how many words are required, and what information and procedures we need to recall. Unfortunately, most students and teachers spend the bulk of their days in this state, which is why schools tend toward an authoritarian approach to education; collaboration both creates and requires a calmer emotional state.
- **Alarm.** Once we are in a state of alarm, it is harder for us to control our emotions, and our thinking and learning become inflexible, reactive, and concrete. When we are alarmed, we are on autopilot—we no longer think, we react. Working with students in this state tends to be very difficult, if not impossible. Expert support may be needed.
- **Fear.** In this state, our thinking becomes almost totally reflexive and centered in the survival system. It becomes difficult for us to hear or even recognize

those around us. When students are in a state of terror—for example, during a schoolyard fight—they often have a vacant look in their eyes. Intervention is usually required for dealing with students in this state.

The chart in Figure 1 shows the types of behavior and thinking expected for each state on the continuum, along with the area of the brain most affected by each state.

FIGURE 1: **Characteristics, Neurological Loci, and Types of Thinking for the Primary Emotional States**

Emotional State	Characteristics	Neurological Loci	Types of Thinking
Calm	• Engaged • Clear-thinking	Neocortex and limbic system	• Higher-order • Problem-solving • Self-regulated and in control
Arousal	• Vigilant • Cautious	Subcortex and limbic system	• Emotional • Concrete
Alarm	• Fearful	Limbic system and survival system	• Automatic
Fear	• Aggressive • Seemingly removed from reality	Survival system	• Strictly reflexive

Individual students will differ in their responses to states of alarm or fear. Some are aggressive; they will confront or act out. Others—usually the quiet students who spend most of their days in the back of the room—appear passive, often withdrawing into fantasies and daydreams. There is a danger that teachers may not recognize this withdrawal as a powerful emotional reaction because it does not result in obvious disruptive behavior. If left unaddressed, however, extreme passivity can ultimately have drastic and even tragic consequences when students realize their more violent fantasies.

Causes and Symptoms of Brain Hijackings

Triggers for brain hijackings include the following:

- Attacks on one's physical appearance.
- Attacks on one's beliefs or values.
- Violations of cultural or accepted customs.

A brain hijacking usually feels like being trapped in a cascade of repetitive and uncontrollable thoughts and emotions that can take the place of clear thinking. Emotions such as anger, fear, or a sense of helplessness can overwhelm those who feel them, leaving them no longer receptive to outside suggestions and unable to think logically. When students' brains are hijacked, they

- React to things reflexively rather than thoughtfully.
- Become humorless or use sarcasm.
- Become more short-tempered than usual.
- Are defensive in situations that don't really warrant it.

In these situations, reframe your own thinking by moving toward a more collaborative mind-set and tone; this will help forestall the stonewalling that confrontation can invite. Guide students through the APA process by

- Maintaining mutual respect.
- Establishing privacy.
- Using nonjudgmental listening.
- Staying calm.
- Knowing when an issue is beyond your ability and expertise.

Examples of Brain Hijackings and How to Deal with Them

Example 1: *A student who is usually friendly and talkative is suddenly withdrawn and uncommunicative. When you address her, she pretends not to hear. You recognize her behavior as an emotional response even though you do not understand why it is happening. The student is responding passively to a state of arousal or alarm.*

What to Do: Reframe—take a deep breath and try to remain as nonjudgmental as possible. In private—perhaps out in the hallway—ask the student if something is wrong and express your concern for her well-being. Do not suggest an explanation for the student's actions, which is for her to disclose. If the student doesn't want to talk, thank her anyway and tell her that you will remain available should she change her mind.

At this point, these are the only steps you can really take. Let your student see your concern and let her go. Move on to the APA process only if the student appears responsive to your intervention.

Example 2: *A student who usually loves class discussion is suddenly belligerent and argumentative. You are disturbed by his comments and get angry.*

What to Do: Reframe—take a deep breath. Try to avoid getting angry and responding in an authoritarian way. The student is reacting aggressively to a state of arousal or alarm by being inflexible and reactive. You recognize this as unusual behavior because the student is usually open-minded and cooperative. Wait until the situation is somewhat defused before asking if there is a problem. Seek privacy before beginning any discussion with the student. Ask questions gently, and only begin the APA process if the student is being honest and direct with you.

Example 3: *Two girls who are usually good friends are suddenly angry with each other. Their anger spills over into your class, with each of them putting down the other. You know that this behavior needs to stop before it escalates. The girls are no longer paying attention to you or the class. They are in a state of alarm, which you recognize because they are highly* *emotional and their comments reflect reactive, inflexible, and concrete thinking.*

What to Do: Reframe—remain calm and ask the students to join you outside the classroom. It is absolutely fair to ask them to stop right now or to separate them. Tell them that you are concerned about the other students and cannot allow them to continue fighting. Do not listen to their accusations; instead, set a time for discussing the situation with them and helping them to resolve their differences. If necessary, help them to make an appointment with a mediator or counselor. Sometimes fights among classmates resolve themselves, so allow a day or two to elapse before meeting with the students.

Additional Considerations When Dealing with Students' Brain Hijackings

- Know when to refer students to someone other than yourself for intervention. Have a list of resources at hand for this purpose. Students with drug or alcohol problems, especially, should get the assistance of educators trained specifically to deal with such issues.
- Know when a situation requires students to use higher-order functions such as decision making, thinking through consequences, or self-understanding. Encourage your students to develop these capacities.
- Use the APA process whenever it is appropriate. Model how to deal with emotional issues in general and provide examples of how to use the APA process for greater self-understanding.

How Different Types of Students React to Their Emotions

Although the APA process works for all students, the causes that lead to brain hijackings vary profoundly depending on whether students are male or female and whether they're in elementary, middle, or high school.

Male Students Versus Female Students

Though we hesitate to generalize too greatly about differences between boys and girls, female students tend to give their emotions verbal expression, whereas male students tend to express themselves more often through action. In addition, boys tend to require more time than girls to identify their emotions. You may want to lead your female students into taking action when appropriate and allow your male students time to identify their feelings. Both boys and girls must be urged to learn about themselves and others, to determine their goals, and to act accordingly.

Elementary School and Early Childhood

Early on, a child's world consists of learning rules and figuring out how things work. Emotions are central, and children's feelings are easily hurt. To young children, "right" and "wrong" are very real absolutes, and they look to adults to enforce them. Because the higher-order thinking or executive skills of young children are developing slowly, adults need to offer them choices within discrete parameters. The ability of young children to reason is limited, and they learn best through routines, clear directions, and consistent follow-through. Making decisions based on rules spelled out by adults may be difficult, but it is important.

Middle School or Preadolescence

Figuring out issues that can't always be reduced to "right" or "wrong" can be confusing to middle school students. There are also many other issues that can confuse them, distract them, and prevent them from achieving academically—issues like making friends and trying out new identities. Students don't always take things too seriously at this age, so teachers need a functioning sense of humor. Remember that these kids are in the process of trying things out, so it's important that you listen and provide them with options.

High School or Adolescence

Adolescents need opportunities to gain social and emotional skills that function as a critical bridge to adulthood. These higher-order or executive skills include

- Monitoring one's emotions.
- Analyzing situations in order to make intelligent decisions.
- Planning for the future.
- Organizing and sequencing.
- Seeing things in perspective.
- Developing a clear sense of identity.

Of all these skills, developing a clear sense of identity is probably the most important for students in high school, who can have particularly negative reactions to having their beliefs about themselves called into question. Landing in an emotional whirlpool due to a hijacked brain can make it impossible for students to practice their executive skills. Although you may not be a therapist, neglecting to help students confront their negative emotions can actually interfere with their acquisition of vital skills.

Using the APA Method with Elementary School Students

Elementary school students believe in rules and in the wisdom of adult authority figures. They have strict codes of fairness and seek approval when they do the right thing. The following types of situations can lead to their brains being hijacked by negative emotions:

- Perceived violations of their notion of fairness.
- Rule breaking.
- The failure of adult authority figures to provide answers to questions or solutions to dilemmas.
- Perceived lack of adult approval for doing the right thing.

Example 1: Suffering Unfairness

Sue is upset because it appears that Carrie took her idea for a project. She and Carrie have worked together on projects before, but Carrie has always given Sue credit for her efforts. Carrie says she had the idea first. Sue is almost in tears and not sure what to do.

As always, begin by reframing. Take a breath and calm down enough to remember that your relationship with your students comes first. Next, apply the APA method:

- **Step 1: Acknowledge.** Deal with the student's physical reaction. Younger children need for you, the authority figure, to respond in the moment—so be prepared for Sue to come to you for help right away. This is the time to help her calm down. Take Sue aside and check on how she is doing. Does she need to take a few deep breaths? Would it help for her to sit by herself or take a short walk? Let her know that you recognize that she is upset. Have her recount what she thinks has happened. Help her stick to the facts as much as possible and repeat them back to her so that both of you are clear.

- **Step 2: Process.** Help the student deal with her emotions by addressing them openly and offering your support. Perhaps Sue is afraid that she can no longer trust Carrie and may lose her as a friend. Or perhaps Sue can't fully articulate what she's feeling. Really try to listen: why is the situation with Carrie such a big deal for her? Though her problems may seem trivial to you, remember that they are not at all trivial to Sue, so watch your tone and demeanor.

Help Sue to identify her options by reviewing the facts of the situation with her. In this case, the key event is out of character for Carrie, who has always honored Sue's contributions in the past. Did Sue come up with the idea on her own, or did she and Carrie both come up with it?

Talk Sue through all the possible solutions to her dilemma and let her decide which might best work for her. In this case, possible solutions might include talking with Carrie, vowing not to work with her in the future, or adopting a more collaborative approach to the project.

- **Step 3: Act.** Help the student take action. If Sue decides to talk with Carrie, you may want to remain a part of the process; if so, be prepared to deal with another cycle of the APA method during recess or lunch. After the student has taken action, check back to see how things worked out. This follow-through can help foster positive relationships with all the students involved and shows confidence in Sue's ability to solve her own problems in the future.

Take an opportunity for additional learning. Challenging a student's idea of fairness can support student development of self-regulation and problem-solving skills. However, be aware that the issue moves beyond your domain once the students have others, including parents, take sides with them in the conflict.

Example 2: Losing Faith in Authority

Students in your class are excited: they've gotten approval from the principal to bring their pets in for Show and Tell on Friday. Suddenly, on Thursday, the principal tells you that the district has decided not to allow the event after all, citing health and safety concerns. Your students and their families are very upset; some parents had even taken time off from work to help students bring their pets in.

Reframe. This is a time for collaboration and healing. Controlling your own reaction is important, so choose your words carefully. When you are prepared, apply the APA method:

- **Step 1: Acknowledge.** Younger students may benefit by venting their frustration over the situation in a physical way. Consider asking the whole class to stand up and shout or jump up and down to relieve tension.
- **Step 2: Process.** Have students sit in a circle, then share what you have been told by the principal and have the students share whatever they know, too. Some students may be looking to blame or put down others; help them to stay on track by reminding them of the facts. Without casting blame, be honest about your own disappointment as well. The key is to remain as orderly and calm as possible. One option for processing the situation in this scenario is to have students write letters to their parents explaining the

reasoning behind the cancellation of Show and Tell. Whatever you decide to do, agree to an action plan and take the time to follow through with it.

- **Step 3: Act.** If you ask your students to write letters to their parents, you can model by writing your own letter and sharing it. Have students collaborate and check one another's grammar. Suspend other assignments; if there is time remaining at the end of the period, do something fun. The next day, follow up by asking your students how their families responded to the letters. Celebrate the collaborative process of finding a solution that worked for everyone.

Take an opportunity for additional learning. When students' faith in authority is challenged, you might engage them in discussions on why we have rules. The issue has moved beyond your domain if the principal disapproves of your actions or if parents become angry and complain.

Example 3: Seeking Approval

T.J. has arrived at school dressed in an outfit that his grandmother made for him, and some of the boys have made fun of him. He wants to fit in, but is confused and very withdrawn as he enters the class.

Reframe to avoid dwelling on the thoughtless behavior of your students. You don't want to have a reflexive response to T.J.'s situation. T.J. needs to be heard, not defended—if you stick up for him too forcefully, he risks losing face in front of others. Apply the APA method:

- **Step 1: Acknowledge.** Let T.J. know that you see that he is upset. Take him aside and ask him if he needs a few moments by himself or if he wants to talk to you or to a friend. If he seems willing, invite T.J. to discuss what has happened. He may be too embarrassed to share much with you, so don't push; let him know you are there for him whenever he is ready to talk. Another option is to share what you have observed or heard with T.J. If necessary, have him repeat what happened.

- **Step 2: Process.** Let T.J. know it's OK for him to feel whatever he is feeling. It might help to share a story of a time when you felt similar emotions. What did you do when everyone laughed after your pants split down the middle? Or the time you showed up to a fancy event in a T-shirt and shorts?

    Consider the consequences of every possible solution to T.J.'s dilemma. Thinking about what could happen as a result of our actions is important for all of us and helps us avert further brain hijackings.

- **Step 3: Act.** If T.J. wants your support, provide it—but let him pick his own way and time to react. When you follow up with T.J., find out if he's still having a problem. If he's not, keep your eye on him and let it go. The simple act of following up will demonstrate that you are sincerely interested in him and his well-being; no further actions may be required.

Take an opportunity for additional learning. Challenges related to seeking approval from classmates provide you with an occasion to support students' development of self-worth. The situation has moved beyond your domain if the student becomes either overly emotional or withdrawn or if his classmates continue to bully him.

Using the APA Method with Middle School Students

Preadolescents are constantly trying out new behaviors and identities. Though natural, this process can often be confusing to students, who are beginning to notice that what their parents want for them and what their peers see as cool often conflict. Resolving this conflict is essential for students to develop their own authentic identities. The following situations commonly trigger brain hijackings among middle school students:

- A sense of loneliness or not fitting in.
- Insecurity about how to act around peers.
- Conflicts with parents and family.
- Being subjected to bullying or cruelty.

Example 1: Feeling Lonely

When Jon enters your classroom, he's visibly upset. Halfway through a basketball game with friends, he realized that the ball had never been passed to him. When he asked his teammate why this was, he got the reply, "You can't hit the basket. We wanted to win."

Begin by reframing. Take a breath and remember not to overreact. Your student needs you to be calm. Then, apply the APA method:

- **Step 1: Acknowledge.** Let Jon know that you understand that he is upset. Show him respect by doing this privately, away from his classmates. Give him a few minutes to settle down; give him some options, like taking a few deep breaths or going for a short walk outside the room. Do your best to help Jon recover privately.

  Get the facts about the situation from Jon, or share with him what you've learned. If you have already built a strong relationship with Jon, he'll probably be straightforward with you. In any case, be sure to encourage him to tell his story, staying strictly to the facts.

- **Step 2: Process.** Help Jon to deal with his hijacked brain by showing your interest in his feelings. Remember, you are not a counselor, you are a teacher, and you are trying to help Jon overcome his negative emotions so that he'll be able to function in class. Help him see that he has options. Ask Jon if he can think of any solutions to his problem, and be prepared to provide some solutions of your own (for example, you could suggest that he join another basketball team, or that he enlist friends to help him practice shooting baskets). Once Jon has reviewed his options, help him choose one that he believes will result in a positive outcome. Whatever option he chooses, help him to examine all the possible consequences.

- **Step 3: Act.** When Jon has decided on a course of action, help him to undertake it and ask him to report how it goes. Write yourself a reminder to ask him about the situation after an appropriate amount of time has passed. Check in with Jon privately. Whether or not his approach to the problem succeeds, he won't forget that you took the time to see how things worked out.

Take an opportunity for additional learning. In situations such as Jon's, consider helping students to discover their unique skills, accept their own limitations, and respect one another's contributions. The issue has moved beyond your domain if it continues to escalate or if the student's parents react poorly to your interventions.

Example 2: Flouting Authority

Sarah is 13 and has been a great student up until now. Suddenly, she is starting to pout in class and act out whenever you ask her to do something. She and her friends appear to be more interested in boys than classwork, though you are aware that Sarah's parents have forbidden her to date until she is at least 16.

Reframe. Take a deep breath and get calm. Stay as non-judgmental as possible as you head into the APA method:

- **Step 1: Acknowledge.** Take Sarah aside and be honest with her about how her actions are affecting her classwork without assigning any blame or showing resentment. If you know about "I" messages and active-listening techniques, this is a great time to use them. Consider whether Sarah could use some time alone to write out her thoughts, take a few deep breaths, or talk over her situation. Really try to listen to Sarah's side of things and share with her your own observations. Bear in mind that being overly dramatic is one of the side effects of this age, so try to keep her focused on how her behavior is affecting her work. Sometimes that is all that is needed.

- **Step 2: Process.** Sarah tells you that she is afraid that her friends will not like her when they discover that she's not allowed to date until she's older. She wants to prove to herself and to her parents that she is responsible enough to date. Here, your listening is very important; you need to let Sarah know that you understand her dilemma and how she feels about it. Share with her options that make sense. She could tell her friends the truth, for example, or work out some acceptable way to attend coed parties with parental guidance, or strive to be helpful and responsible at home and school so that her parents can see her growing into an adult. Sarah will need to decide what will work for her. Talk over the options and all the possible consequences. This will help her to see that every action has a reaction.

- **Step 3: Act.** Support Sarah's decisions; if you need to be involved further, let her know what you are willing to do. There is no better way to ensure that students know they are being heard than checking back with them after a reasonable amount of time. Keep reminders in your calendar to do just that.

Take an opportunity for additional learning. When attending to students who are flouting authority, see this as a chance to help them develop the ability to make hard choices and manage strong emotions. You know that the situation has moved beyond your domain if the student continues acting out inappropriately in class or requires professional counseling.

Example 3: Being Bullied

When you notice that the usually bubbly and outgoing Monica has suddenly become withdrawn, you suspect that she's being bullied or teased.

Start by reframing. Bullying is a very sensitive issue. Take care to come across as collaborative rather than authoritarian. Apply the APA method:

- **Step 1: Acknowledge.** Take Monica aside for a talk. Remember to always show the student respect by not confronting her in front of her peers. Tell Monica what you've observed and ask her what's going on. Ask her if she wants to meet with a counselor or if she just needs some time to think about what is going on. See if she feels free to talk with you. If she does, get the facts as she sees them. As it turns out, Monica has received some text messages from an unidentified number calling her a nasty word. Though counseling may be called for, your willingness to listen and offer support will also prove to be important.

- **Step 2: Process.** Help Monica deal with her emotions. What options does she have? She can delete any offensive text messages immediately, or perhaps go see a counselor. Help Monica to consider the consequences of whatever course of action she selects.
- **Step 3: Act.** Help Monica to act. If she chooses to see a counselor, help her do so. Be especially sure to follow up with students when bullying is an issue. One of the worst things about preadolescence is the feeling of isolation and rejection that it invites. It might be a good idea to talk with the counselor yourself to see if he or she can recommend some approaches you might use in future cases of bullying.

Make sure that the administration knows what is going on and is taking steps to address it. Many districts provide support programs intended for bullying situations. Other approaches that may help include

- Setting up antibullying committees or groups.
- Providing parents and students with a handbook detailing school safety policies that they are required to sign off on.
- Developing social media codes of conduct to encourage civility on the Internet.

Take an opportunity for additional learning. Bullying situations provide you with the opportunity to involve students in brainstorming ways to reduce bullying and show respect for others. The situation has moved beyond your domain if the bullies don't cease their behavior or if the bullied student's withdrawal worsens.

Using the APA Method with High School Students

Because the adolescent brain can be hijacked on a daily basis by issues that end up resolving themselves quickly, judging the seriousness of a given situation can be difficult for educators and parents alike. You must decide when to follow the steps of the APA method and when to simply wait out the situation.

As we've already discussed, higher-order thinking skills play a critical role in managing emotions. These skills first manifest themselves in adolescence—they tend to fully develop roughly between the ages of 10 and 27—and require ongoing practice to remain sharp. High school is the time for students to practice

- Applying problem-solving skills.
- Gathering data that can inform decisions.

- Developing a sense of self that is largely independent of others' opinions.
- Being guided by lessons learned from challenges, mistakes, and feedback.
- Valuing the logic and opinions of experts.
- Recognizing and admitting their own shortcomings.
- Understanding their own emotions and the emotions of others.

Teachers and parents can get very confused by teenage behavior, which is often erratic and strange. The good news is that adolescents can now actually—finally!—see the consequences of their own actions. They are beginning to distinguish between risks and opportunities, both of which require them to engage with others. The skills that students develop in high school are essential to balancing emotional reactions and sophisticated academic work. Too often, schools ignore the teaching of social and complex cognitive skills in favor of memorization and replication. Developing more complex skills requires exposure to unfamiliar thinking and problem-solving strategies. Though spending time on emotional issues can be frustrating to teachers, it's important to recognize the damage that brain hijackings can do to the kind of higher-order skills that teenagers need to develop.

Relationship issues are different for high school students, whose academic pressures can leave little time for in-depth social interactions with peers. Navigating the turbulent emotions of adolescence can help students acquire the skills they will need to develop their executive function. The concerns that can lead to hijacking by such emotions include

- Body image issues.
- Pressure to excel academically.
- Pressure to own the latest technology.
- Conflict with parents' religious or moral beliefs.
- Issues related to romance and sex.
- Popularity issues.
- Financial pressures.

Confusion and emotional upheavals can easily overwhelm young people. Without healthy, respectful relationships with adults, the temptation to escape can become too much for them to handle. Vulnerable adolescents can be easily led to experiment with substances like alcohol or drugs, potentially leading to serious long-term harm. Young adults don't have the necessary discernment that comes with fully developed decision-making skills. As a result, they all too frequently have upsetting reactions at the very time they desperately need to develop emotional balance and control. Adolescents need and want to solve problems on their own.

Example 1: Dealing with Body Image Issues

Brandon knows that he has been gaining a few pounds but tells himself it is muscle. When you jokingly suggest that he has been hitting the donut shop a little too often, he doesn't think it's funny, even though he laughs along with you and his friends who overhear you. He feels angry and depressed. Even after everyone has forgotten your comment, Brandon can't stop replaying it and his friends' laughter in his head. He is rightfully angry—with you!

Reframe. Keep calm and observe. Apply the APA method:

- **Step 1: Acknowledge.** Brandon may suddenly turn quiet, ignore you, or maybe do something that he knows will irritate you or is blatantly against the rules. Show him that you notice any changes in behavior.

  Considering the situation, Brandon may not welcome suggestions from you. Consider waiting until after he has had P.E. class to help him process his feelings—physical activity helps to dispel negative emotions. If Brandon's changes in behavior continue, observe him but stay calm and don't ask for an explanation.

- **Step 2: Process.** Take Brandon aside and ask him what is going on. If you don't get an honest answer, ask him if he needs something from you. This may signal to him that you know he's upset about something you said—that you are sensitive and are paying attention to him. At this point, listening is really important in order to repair your relationship.

- **Step 3: Act.** This situation may simply require an apology from you to Brandon. It doesn't even have to be explicit; for example, it could come in the form of singling out his work in class. Try to get Brandon involved in doing things that he's good at. Remember that his sense of self has been temporarily damaged, and one way to repair it is to have him feel confident and competent again as soon as possible.

Take an opportunity for additional learning. Challenges to a student's body image can provide a way for the student to develop a sense of self largely independent of others' opinions. The situation has moved beyond your domain if you suspect that the student might be suffering from anorexia or bulimia.

Example 2: Challenging Beliefs About One's Abilities

Casey feels she is ready to drive a motorcycle. Her parents tell her that she is too young and doesn't have the ability or good judgment it takes to drive a motorcycle responsibly. Casey defends herself to her parents over and over again. In class, Casey doesn't pay attention and is glum and uncooperative. You are puzzled and frustrated with her behavior.

Reframe. Recognize that you may be dealing with a case of parental disapproval. Remain nonjudgmental and refrain from saying too much. Then, begin the APA method:

- **Step 1: Acknowledge.** Take Casey aside and ask her what is going on. Tell her what you've observed in neutral language free of blame. If you have a trusting relationship with Casey, she may tell you what is happening. However, she will not share anything with you if she feels that you are judging her or that you may betray her trust by talking to her parents.

- **Step 2: Process.** Share with Casey what you have observed and simply tell her what you need from her. Ask her how she can help both of you resolve the situation. Come up with some possible options to share with Casey. For example, could she take some formal motorcycle driving lessons that her parents would approve of? Can she learn something from statistics on adolescent driving? Be specific and stick to actions you can both document.
- **Step 3: Act.** Follow up with Casey and see if she needs anything else. Chances are that simply paying attention to her will be enough to improve your relationship.

Take an opportunity for additional learning. When working with students whose beliefs about their abilities have been challenged, help them research the actual facts. These can inform students and their parents alike on how to address the situation. The situation has moved beyond your domain if the student defiantly takes to driving a motorcycle in secret or if her home life veers out of control.

Example 3: Performing Below Expectations

Karen is a history buff and prides herself on her knowledge of United States history. Her grades have always been above average, until the day she receives a C+ for a paper she had worked hard on. She is incredulous, angry, and hostile, and she wants an explanation from you.

Start by reframing. Stay calm and wait for Karen to finish making her case. Refrain from reacting to her anger as much as possible. If necessary, seek out a cooling-off period. Apply the APA method:

- **Step 1: Acknowledge.** Karen might greet any advice from you with hostility, given that she sees you as being at the root of her problem. Ask her to write out her specific complaints; this will give her time to fume—and, once calm, to think.
- **Step 2: Process.** When Karen gives you her written complaints, tell her that you will respond either in writing or during a meeting. Approach Karen's complaints one at a time. Take notice if you find that at any point you can't defend your grading of her paper. Be willing to admit mistakes. Remember that you are modeling behavior, so your reactions count for a lot. Provide Karen with some options for resolving the situation that both of you can live with.
- **Step 3: Act.** Follow through with Karen to make sure that the original breach between you is healing.

Take an opportunity for additional learning. When working with students who perform below expectations, see this as an opportunity to help them come to terms with differing standards. This approach can help students recognize their shortcomings, value the opinions of others, and develop a greater sense of control over academic matters. The situation has moved beyond your domain if the student is abusive toward you or if she simply insists on a better grade.

Example 4: Having Allegiances Challenged

Lee is an avid football player and identifies very strongly with his team, which is not doing as well as it has in the past. He overhears someone refer to the team as "those losers," and it takes all the self-control he can muster not to confront the guy. He is in no mood for his classes. You find him truculent and sarcastic and are often shocked by his behavior.

Begin by reframing. Stay calm; try to model understanding and patience as you move into the APA method.

- **Step 1: Acknowledge.** You have to let Lee know that you have observed the change in his behavior. He seems angry to you, and you'd like to know why. Ask him if anything is wrong and, if so, whether there's anything you can do to help. Ask him to take time out to think or to do something physical to get his mind off the situation. Depending on the relationship you have developed with Lee over time, he may or may not share with you the extent of his feelings. If he does tell you his story, show genuine sympathy but help him stick to the facts as much as possible.
- **Step 2: Process.** What does Lee need from you at this time? Consider suggesting that he write a letter to the school newspaper in defense of his team. Even if he doesn't submit it, writing it can help to release his frustrations. Have him select a course of action.
- **Step 3: Act.** Make sure that Lee follows through with his course of action by checking back in with him until the matter is resolved.

Take an opportunity for additional learning. When you work with students who find their allegiances challenged, see this as a chance to help them develop a healthy sense of independence and clarify their own unique beliefs and values. The situation has moved beyond your domain if the student attacks anyone physically or if his behavior becomes too disruptive to bear.

A Final Word

For parents and educators alike, helping students to deal with emotional issues while they're also supposed to be focusing on academic achievement can be very challenging. However, if students don't learn early on how to master their emotions, they will have a hard time in the future and may be robbed of a chance to master essential life skills. In this technology-driven world, the future belongs to those students who have developed the social and emotional skills essential to working with others. The ability to tolerate emotional pressures and connect across cultures will open many doors.

Tests alone can't assess the types of higher-order thinking, problem solving, critical discernment, and analysis essential to any successful adult interaction. Allowing your students the time and space to process their emotional reactions in a healthy way is crucial. Students need to master the ability to *acknowledge* emotions (their own and others'), to *process* and learn from their emotions, and to *act* by implementing solutions that address emotional challenges successfully.

To give your feedback on this publication and be entered into a drawing for a free ASCD Arias e-book, please visit **www.ascd.org/ariasfeedback**

ASCD | arias™

ENCORE

DEALING WITH WHOLE-CLASS DISRUPTIONS

Sometimes, emotional situations develop that engulf the whole class. This can often occur in the aftermath of unexpected tragedies or natural disasters. Attempting to ignore such disruptions will only compound the turmoil they stir up. It is crucial that you remain calm and able to function, so take a deep breath and begin by implementing some of the suggestions below.

Sharing feelings: You will have to establish a method for letting students express their emotions in class. Consider using a talking stick or Ordered Sharing (see www.nlri.org) to ensure that each person's voice is heard. The Ordered Sharing format allows students to develop the skills of non-judgmental listening (to oneself and others), patience, and open-mindedness. In our classes, we've had students do things like write letters to victims of national tragedies, plan how to deal with emergencies, and create a fund to help those in distress.

Examining the chain of escalating conflict: This involves looking at what happened—a fight on the playground, say—and retracing the steps that led up to it. Whenever we've had students do this, we've found that they were able to identify multiple opportunities for intervention before the event. Retracing steps in this way helps your students to see just how rapidly actions can escalate.

Seeking consensus: Teaching students to come to agreement over conflicts that affect the whole class is an excellent way to build community and avoid frustration. We recommend using the quick-check "fist to five" voting method, which requires the whole class to work together toward a solution. Ask students to signal how they feel about proposed ideas by having them raise

- A fist: "I don't accept the idea, but I can offer an alternative."
- One finger: "I can live with the idea, but I have serious concerns or questions."
- Two fingers: "I can accept this idea, but I have some reservations."
- Three fingers: "I'm OK with this idea, but I'm not overjoyed."
- Four fingers: "This is a good idea."
- Five fingers: "Wow, this is a great idea!"

Developing self-awareness: "I" messages: It is very important to let people know how you or your students are feeling about a difficult situation and that you/they would like to work it out. What is said and how it is said needs to be encouraging and inviting to the other person without blaming or threatening. "I" messages ask an individual to express what he or she is feeling and thinking. Below is a simple formula for expressing "I" messages without sounding stilted. With practice, this will become natural. Remember that any method we want students to learn needs to be modeled by us.

"I" messages format:

- "WHEN" must be as neutral as you can make it. Say, "When this situation occurs," not "When you do this . . ." The second response sounds like blaming.
- "I FEEL" should be followed by one word that expresses an emotion, such as happy, sad, mad, or glad. Do not say, "I feel like . . ."
- "I WANT" shows your willingness to work out the problem. It should not be said in a demanding way or with the expectation that you will get everything you want.
- "I AM WILLING" lets the other person know what it will take to make you feel OK again and that negotiations are open.

Put together, these phrases form an effective "I" message: **When** [this situation occurs], **I feel** [an emotion]. **I want** [what it will take to make things better]. **I am willing** [to do what I can to make things better].

Remember:

"You" messages escalate the conflict, invite attack and blame, and create defensiveness. They make collaboration impossible.

"I" messages de-escalate the conflict, focus on the feelings of the speaker, and invite collaboration.

References

Goleman, D. (2001). *Emotional intelligence: Why it can matter more than IQ*. New York: Bantam Books.

Perry, B. D. (2003, Oct. 8). Workshop at the Second Annual Southwest Family Violence Conference presented by the Alternatives to Domestic Violence and Prevent Child Abuse Council of Southwest Riverside County, CA.

Related Resources

At the time of publication, the following ASCD resources were available (ASCD stock numbers appear in parentheses). For up-to-date information about ASCD resources, go to www.ascd.org. You can search the complete archives of *Educational Leadership* at http://www.ascd.org/el.

ASCD EDge©
Exchange ideas and connect with other educators on the social networking site ASCD EDge at http://ascdedge.ascd.org/

Print Products
Connecting with Students by Allen N. Mendler (#101236)

Discipline with Dignity, 3rd Edition: New Challenges, New Solutions by Richard L. Curwin, Allen N. Mendler, and Brian D. Mendler (#108036)

The Educator's Guide to Preventing and Solving Discipline Problems by Mark Boynton and Christine Boynton (#105124)

Hanging In: Strategies for Teaching the Students Who Challenge Us Most by Jeffrey Benson (#114013)

Inspiring the Best in Students by Jonathan C. Erwin (#110006)
Winning Strategies for Classroom Management by Carol J. Cummings (#100052)

ASCD PD Online© Courses
Classroom Management: Building Effective Relationships, 2nd Ed. (#PD11OC104)
Classroom Management: Managing Challenging Behavior, 2nd Ed. (#PD14OC015)

For more information: send e-mail to member@ascd.org; call 1-800-933-2723 or 703-578-9600, press 2; send a fax to 703-575-5400; or write to Information Services, ASCD, 1703 N. Beauregard St., Alexandria, VA 22311-1714 USA.

About the Authors

Renate Caine has taught middle school in Reno, Nevada, and high school in New Orleans, Louisiana, and helped to establish a small charter school in her local community. She received her Ph.D. from the University of Florida, where her dissertation revealed that teachers' use of "I" messages and active-listening strategies in the classroom positively affected students' self-concepts and attitude toward school and teachers after only six months of use. She recently retired from 20 years as a college professor and is currently the executive director of the Natural Learning Research Institute (www.nlri.org). She is the coauthor of the original ASCD publication *Making Connections: Teaching and the Human Brain* and nine others. By employing many of the strategies in this publication over the years, Renate eliminated almost all discipline problems, and her students have won awards for their high academic achievement. She can be reached at renate@nlri.org.

Carol McClintic taught for 35 years in the public education system, from preschool to university extension classes. She received her Bachelor of Science degree from South Dakota State University and her Master of Arts degree from California State University, San Bernardino (CSUSB). She was part of her District Leadership Team and conducted many workshops for the district and for the University of California, Riverside; the University of California, Los Angeles; and CSUSB on topics such as conflict resolution. As an elementary and middle school teacher, she initiated use of the APA method discussed in these pages and saw immediate results: not only did her students' discipline problems disappear, but her students also developed valuable skills in managing their emotions and handling social situations.

She began working with Renate and Geoffrey Caine in 1992 with a five-year restructuring grant for a new middle school and was a senior associate with Caine Learning. Presently she is the director of programs for educators and independent learning for the Natural Learning Research Institute (www.nlri.org) as well as the secretary/treasurer for the NLRI Board of Directors. She can be reached at info@nlri.org.